Jav

JavaScript Programming for Beginners Guide to JavaScript Coding, JavaScript Programs and JavaScript Language

By

Josh Thompsons

This document is geared towards providing exact and reliable information in regards to the topic and issue covered. The publication is sold with the idea that the publisher is not required to render accounting, officially permitted, or otherwise, qualified services. If advice is necessary, legal or professional, a practiced individual in the profession should be ordered.

- From a Declaration of Principles which was accepted and approved equally by a Committee of the American Bar Association and a Committee of Publishers and Associations.

The information provided herein is stated to be truthful and consistent, in that any liability, in terms of inattention or otherwise, by any usage or abuse of any policies, processes, or directions contained within is the solitary and utter responsibility of the recipient reader. Under no circumstances will any legal responsibility or blame be held against the publisher for any reparation, damages, or

JavaScript

Contents

◇Introduction 6

◇Setting Up Your Environment 7

◇Introduction to JavaScript 13

◇Statements 19

◇Comments 25

◇Variables 29

◇Type Conversion 45

◇Operators 55

◇String Operators...67

◇If / else Statements 75

◇Boolean Logic and Switch Statements 81

◇Functions 97

◇Arrays..103

◇JavaScript Array Methods 113

◇Sorting Arrays 125

◇Loops and Iteration 137

◇20 Questions to Test Your JavaScript Knowledge 147

◇Conclusion 153

◇Answers to Exercises 154

◇Answers to JavaScript Quiz 170

Introduction

I want to thank you and congratulate you for purchasing the book, "JavaScript: JavaScript Programming for Beginners Guide to JavaScript Coding, JavaScript Programs and JavaScript Language".

This book is going to help you understand JavaScript, what it is, how it works and what it is used for. JavaScript is one of the lightest and most dynamic of the computer programming languages, with these features:

- Interpreted, lightweight language
- Originally designed for creating applications that are network-centric
- Integrated with and complementary to Java and HTML
- Open-source
- Cross-platform

Unlike most of the other programming languages, JavaScript is a core part of any website and you will find that names such as Google, Bing and Yahoo all run their websites through it.

As a beginner, unless you have looked at any programming language, you will find this confusing, so to help you out, I have included plenty of working examples, exercises for you to do and, as a finish, a multiple-choice quiz to help cement your understanding.

If you are ready, let's step into JavaScript!

Setting Up Your Environment

To begin writing JavaScript you need two things – a good web browser with web development tools and a text editor. For the purposes of this book, we are going to use Google Chrome and Brackets text editor.

Google Chrome

As a newbie to JavaScript, it is important that you learn the console, including setting it up. Google Chrome has a built-in console that is ideal for practicing your JavaScript and it's free. Here's how to get it:

1. Open your web browser and go to www.google.com/Chrome and download it - Once installed, you can decide whether to have this as your main web browser or not. All the instructions for installing are on the screen so follow them carefully

2. In top right corner of the Chrome page, you will see an options circle – click on it and several options will appear

3. Click **More Tools**

4. Click **Developer Tools** and then **Console.** This will show you the console pad and it will have a symbol on it - >. This is the command prompt and is where your code is typed in.

5. Note that there are tools available for enlarging the view and for editing and deleting entries.

You are now ready to start using the Chrome console so spend some time exploring it and working out what everything is and what it all does.

Shortcut Method

A shortcut to opening your console:

1. Once you have downloaded and installed Chrome, go to the address bar and type in **about: blank**

2. This will show you a blank page

Shortcut Commands

Press on CTRL+SHIFT+J – Windows

Press on ALT+J - Mac

Once the console in open follow the instructions above for setting up the console

Getting Started

Now your console is set up you can login in – type console.log() at the command prompt, and begin exploring JavaScript and how it all works. There will be practical examples for you to try throughout the book so keep this open and ready

If you want to preserve what you type in, click on the Preserve Log button on the top right corner of the console.

And, to save, right-click on the console and select Save As.

Brackets

Brackets is an open source text editor designed for web development. Built with JavaScript, it is the ideal editor providing tons of tools and visual help, making your coding experience much simpler and much more effective.

1. Download Brackets from http://brackets.io/ - versions are available for Mac, Windows, and Linux

Getting to Know Brackets

When you first open Brackets, you will see a project called "Getting Started". There are instructions on the screen that provide you with a walkthrough of the features in Brackets.

- To open a folder, click on **File>Open Folder** from the file tree on the left of the screen. This folder will be considered by Brackets to be your projects and it will be the scope for many search operations. There are also a few settings that are tied to it. Switching between projects is simple; just click the name of the root folder in the file tree. You also have the option of dragging a folder from your OS to Brackets, where it will open

- Many text editors show all your open files in tab form but Brackets has a list called "Working Files", located above the tree. If you click a file in the tree, you will just view it but it will not be added to the Working Files list. This makes it easy to browse through the files without having loads of them open. If you make any changes to any file, it will automatically be added to the Working Files list and, if you wanted to put a file on that list without making any edits, simply double-click the name in the file tree.

To start with, you will only see one editor in the main Brackets view but it is possible to split it, showing two editors, either vertically or horizontally. To do this, click on **View** and then choose from **Vertical Split** or **Horizontal Split.** Your main view will now be turned into two, allowing you to see two files at a time. This will also give you another "Working Files" list, showing you which files are open in each of the panes. If you want to move a file from one list to another, simply drag it between them.

One thing Brackets will do is remember which view layout you have for each of your projects. If you go to another project, you will see the layout that was in place when the project was saved and closed. To go back to having just one editor in view, click on **View>No Split.** When you do this, you will not be shutting down the files that were open; instead, the two lists of Working Files will be merged and your changes stored in memory until you save or discard them.

Have a play around with Brackets and, when you are ready, open a new console window and we'll get right into coding.

Introduction to JavaScript

JavaScript consists of programs, which are known as scripts. These scripts can be written directly in the web page HTML and, as the webpage loads up, they are automatically executed. Each script is in plain text, needing no special compilation to run and this is what makes JavaScript different from Java, two languages that are commonly confused.

Why is it Called JavaScript?

When it was first created, JavaScript was called LiveScript but, with the Java language being one of the most popular at the time, the developers decided that a new language was needed as a "baby brother" to Java and, as such JavaScript was born.

Over time, JavaScript became a language in its own right, and is now completely independent to Java, having no relationship whatsoever. At the moment, JavaScript is versatile enough that it can execute in the browser, on a server or on any device that has a program called the JavaScript Engine. The browser has its own engine embedded and is often called the JavaScript Virtual machine. The different engines all have their own codenames, such as V8 for Opera and Chrome, Gecko for Firefox, Squirrelfish and Nitro for Safari, Chakracore for Edge, and so on. You should remember the names because you will often see them referred to in relation to JavaScript. For example, you might see something like "feature Y is supported by V8" and that will give you an indication that it will work on Opera and Chrome.

How Do the Engines Work?

The engines themselves are quite complicated but the basics of them are simple:

- The script gets written as plain text and is distributed as plain text
- The engine which, if in a browser is embedded. Will then read, or parse, the script and convert or compile it into the machine-readable language.
- Then it will run – fast!

At every stage, the engine will apply optimization. It will be watching the script while it is running, analyzing all the data that comes through and using that knowledge to optimize the code.

What Can In-Browser JavaScript Do?

Modern JavaScript is considered to be one of the safest programming languages because it doesn't provide any access, low-level or otherwise, to the CPU or memory. The reason for this is that JavaScript was originally created for use in browsers and these do not require that kind of access level.

The environment that JavaScript is running in will dictate the capabilities. For example, Node.JS will support those functions that let JavaScript and read and write arbitrary files, carry out network requests, and so on. The in-browser JavaScript can do anything that is related to manipulation of web pages, user interaction, and the web server. For example, in-browser JavaScript can:

- React to actions from a user
- Change content on a page
- Add new HTML
- Modify the styles
- Send network requests
- Upload and download files
- Get cookies and set cookies
- As the user questions
- Show the user messages
- Remember browser data

It can't do everything though. In-browser JavaScript is limited to protect the safety of the user, i.e. to stop a malicious web page from accessing their private and confidential date. Restrictions of the in-browser capabilities include:

- Not being able to read or write arbitrary files to a hard drive
- Not being able to copy the files or execute programs
- Not having any access directly to the functions of the operating system
- Although it can work with a file in a modern browser, it only has limited access and that is only if a user does specific things, like selecting a file through an <input> tag or dropping files into the browser window.
- Limited in access to the cameras and/or microphone on a device and that access is only allowed if the user gives express permission. This means that any page run on JavaScript may not enable your webcam or microphone

The different windows and tabs you use are not aware of one another unless JavaScript is used to open a window or tab from another one. Even so, JavaScript that is in one window or a tab cannot access the JavaScript on another if they are from different ports, protocols or domains

This is known as "Same Origin Policy" and the only way around it is for both of the JavaScript pages to have a special code that can handle the exchange of data. Again, this is for the safety of the user, stopping one page from accessing personal details on another.

JavaScript is more than able to communicate with the current page server over the network but it cannot receive data from any other domain or site. It is possible but it must have express permission, through the HTTP headers on the web page and that must be granted from the remote side. Again, user safety is paramount.

However, if JavaScript is out of the browser, such as on a server, there are no limits. Modern browsers also let you install extensions and plugins which can have extended permissions. These should be considered carefully before being installed though as some can cause problems for the safety of the user.

Why is JavaScript Unique?

There are three, if not more, things that are so good about JavaScript:

1. It provides full HTML/CSS integration
2. It makes simple things simple to do
3. It has support for all the biggest browsers and is already enabled by default

You will not find these three features combined in any browser technology except for JavaScript and that is why it is so unique and why it is the widest-used method of creating a browser interface.

Now that you have a better understanding of how JavaScript works, it's time to start looking into the language itself. Have Google Chrome Console or Brackets Text editor open and ready.

Statements

Statements in JavaScript are kind of like a set of instructions that the web browser will execute. The following statement is telling the browser to write "Hello Harry: in an HTML element using id="demo":

```
document.getElementById("demo").innerHTML = "Hello Harry.";
```

JavaScript Programs

Most programs in JavaScript will contain several statements. Each of these statements will be executed, one at a time, in the order they are written in. For example, we give variables x, y, and z each a value and then display z:

```
var x, y, z;
x = 7;
y = 8;
z = x + y;
document.getElementById("demo").innerHTML = z;
```

Another name for these programs and statements is JavaScript code.

<u>Using Semicolons (;)</u>

Semicolons are used to separate statements and one should be input between each statement that is to be executed:

var a, b, c;
a = 7;
b = 8;
c = a + b;
When you use the semicolon, you can place several statements on one line:

a = 7; b = 8; c = a + b;

White Space

Multiple spaces are ignored in JavaScript so white space can be included in your script so it is easier to read. Look at the following lines – each means the same but the first is easier to read:

var person = "Hege";
var person="Hege";

It is good practice to add spaces around each operator - =, +, -, /, *:

var x = y + z;

Line Length and Line Breaks

To make your script truly readable, you should try to avoid using more than 80 characters in each of your code lines. If you can't fit your statement on one line, you must break it and the best place is following an operator, like this:

```
document.getElementById("demo").innerHTML =
"Hello Harry.";
```

JavaScript Code Blocks

You can group statements together in blocks of code, inside a set of curly brackets. The purpose of these code blocks is to define all the statements that are to execute together. One of the places that you will find these blocks of statements grouped together is in a JavaScript function:

```
function myFunction() {
    document.getElementById("demo1").innerHTML = "Hello Harry.";
    document.getElementById("demo2").innerHTML = "Are you well?";
}
```

JavaSript Keywords

Earlier, I mentioned keywords. A statement generally starts with a keyword that will identify which action is to be done. These are some of the keywords and what they mean:

Keyword	Description
break	used to terminate loops or switches
continue	exits a loop and goes back to the top
debugger	halts the code execution and, if it is available, calls the debugging function
do ... while	used to execute statement blocks, repeating the block while a specified condition evaluates true
for	marks a statement block that is going to be executed, so long as a specified condition evaluates true
function	used for declaring functions
if ... else	marks a statement block for execution, dependent on specified conditions
return	will exit out of a function
switch	marks a statement block for execution, dependent on the different cases

try ... catch   used to implement error handling for a
specified statement block

var   used for declaring variables

These keywords are reserved which means they cannot be used for anything other than their purpose. One thing you definitely must not do is use a reserved keyword when you name a variable.

Comments

Comments are used to describe what is happening in a piece of code and to make it easier to read and understand. A comment can also be used to stop code from executing when you are testing out alternative code.

Single Line Comments

A single line comment is denoted by two backslashes - //. Any text that comes after these and up to the end of the line will be ignored and will not be executed by JavaScript.

In this example, we have a single line comment before each line of code:

```
// Change the heading:
document.getElementById("myH").innerHTML = "The First Page";
// Change the paragraph:
document.getElementById("myP").innerHTML = "The first paragraph.";
```

But in this example, we are using the comment at the end of the lines to explain what the code is doing:

```
var x = 7;     // Declare x, and then give it a value of 7
```

var y = x + 3; // Declare y, and then give it a value of x + 2

Multi-line Comments

A multi-line comment is one that goes over more than one line and begins with /*, ending with */. Any text that is written between these will not be executed.

In this example, we are using a multi-line comment, otherwise known as a comment block, to explain what the code is doing:

```
/*
The code underneath is going to change
the heading with the id = "theH"
and the paragraph with the id = "theP"
in the web page:
*/
document.getElementById("myH").innerHTML = "The First Page";
document.getElementById("myP").innerHTML = "The first paragraph.";
```

While multi-line comments are commonly used in formal documentation, we generally

Using a Comment to Prevent Code Execution

This is normally used for code testing. We know that, when you add // to the start of a line, you are changing it from code that can be executed to a comment. In this next example, we are using // to stop one of the lines of code form executing:

//document.getElementById("myH").innerHTML = "The First Page";
document.getElementById("myP").innerHTML = "The first paragraph.";

And in this example, we are using the multiline comment to stop multiple lines form executing:

/*
document.getElementById("myH").innerHTML = "The First Page";
document.getElementById("myP").innerHTML = "The first paragraph.";
*/

Variables

Like any other programming language, a JavaScript variable can be described as a storage box, a place in the memory for storing values. For example:

var x = 4;
var y = 5;
var z = x + y;

x, y, and z are all variables and each has been given a value:

x has the value of 4

y has the value of 5

z has the value of 9

If you are familiar with Algebra then you will be familiar with how this next example works:

var price1 = 4;
var price2 = 5;
var total = price1 + price2;
In computer programming, variables hold values, just as in algebra and, we can use those variables in an expression (total = price1 + price2).

So, the value of the variable called total would be 9.

Identifiers

Every variable in JavaScript must be provided with a name, called an identifier. These are to be unique, may be short or longer with more description. Whatever you name your variables, you must follow a set of naming conventions:

- Use letters a to z or A to Z, numbers 0 to 9, dollar signs ($) and underscores (_). No other symbols may be used
- The name must start with a letter
- Be aware that JavaScript is case sensitive. Variables called a and A are two different variables
- You may not use reserved keywords in names – more about these later

Assignment Operator

Although I will be talking more about operators later, you need to know about this one now. The assignment operator is an equal (=) sign. This is where variables differ from algebra because, in that, = means equal to. Look at the following example; it makes no sense in algebra:

x = x + 6

However, in JavaScript, it does, because it is assigning a value of x + 6 to x, or in simpler terms, it will calculate what x + 6 is and then put the result in x. x's value will be incremented by 6.

Data Types

Be aware that a variable is able to hold values that are of number type and text type. A text value is called a text string and while JavaScript is capable of handling several different data types, for now, we will concentrate on the numbers and the strings.

A text string is enclosed in single or double quotes while a number has no quotes. If you were to enclose a number inside a set of quote marks, it would be seen as a string. For example:

var pi = 3.14;
var person = "Jane Deer";
var answer = 'Yes I can!';

Declaring a JavaScript Variable

When you create a variable, you are declaring it and you do this with the var keyword:

Var carName;

After you declare a variable it will not have any value until you assign it one. To assign values you use the assignment operator (=):

carName = "Ford"

However, you can declare a variable and assign it a value at the same time. In the next example, we are going to declare the variable, carName, assign it a value of "Ford" and then output that value in an HTML paragraph that has id="demo":

```
<p id="demo"></p>
```

```
<script>
var carName = "Ford";
document.getElementById("demo").innerHTML =
carName;
</script>
```

Get into the practice of declaring all the variables you are going to use at the start of your script – this will make life easy for you.

One Statement, Several Variables

You are not limited to one variable per statement; you can use several. Just make sure you begin the statement with the var keyword and then ensure that each variable name is separated by a comma:

```
var person = "Jane Deer", carName = "Ford", price = 300;
```

Each declaration can go over more than one line:

```
var person = "Jane Deer",
carName = "Ford",
price = 300;
```

Undefined Value

In a computer program, it wouldn't be unusual to find a declared variable that has no value. In these cases, the value may be the result of a calculation that has to be done or perhaps something that may be input later, such as something from a user. These variables, although they have no specific value, actually have a value of undefined. After the next statement is executed, the variable called carName will have a value of undefined:

```
var carName;
```

Re-Declaring a Variable

Variables that are re-declared do not lose their initial value. For example, if we re-declared carName, it would retain its vale of "Ford" after the statements are executed:

```
var carName = "Ford";
var carName;
```

Arithmetic

With a JavaScript variable, you can use certain operators that allow you to do arithmetic, such as, + and =. For example:

var x = 3 + 4 + 5;
You are also able to add strings together but these will be concatenated, i.e. joined together. For example:

var x = "Jane" + " " + "Deer";

You could also do this:

var x = "3" + 4 + 5;
If you place a number inside quote marks, the remaining numbers will be seen as strings and they will be concatenated or joined together. Have a go at this:

var x = 1 + 4 + "5";
Data Types

A variable is able to hold several data types, such as strings, numbers, objects, etc.

var length = 15;   // Number
var lastName = "Parker";   // String
var x = {firstName:"Jane", lastName:"Deer"};   // Object

Data types are a very important concept for you to remember in computer programming. If you are going to perform an operation on a variable, you must have some knowledge about the type. Take the following example; without a type, the computer could not solve this safely:

var x = 15 + "Ford";

Does this make any sense? Adding Ford to 15? Would it come up with a result or an error? JavaScript will see this example as"

var x = "15" + "Ford";

When you add a string and a number, JavaScript will see the number as a string. Try this example yourself:

var x = 15 + "Ford";

And this one:

var x = "Ford" + 15;

JavaScript will evaluate any expression from the left to the right and sequences that are different will have results that are different:

var x = 15 + 6 + "Ford";

Result:

21Ford

var x = "Ford" + 15 + 6;

Result:

Ford156

The first example shows JavaScript seeing the numbers 15 and 6 as numbers until it gets to "Ford". The second example shows everything being treated as a string because the first one is a string.

Dynamic Types

Dynamic types are a big part of JavaScript. What this means is that one variable can hold several different data types. For example:

```
var x;          // x is undefined
var x = 6;      // x is a Number
var x = "Jane";    // x is a String
```

Strings

Strings are series of characters, such as "Jane Deer". All strings are enclosed in double or single quotes – please note, you cannot mix these and use, for example, a single quote to open a string and a double quote to close it.

```
var carName = "Ford XS80";  // with double quotes
var carName = 'Ford XS80;   // with single quotes
```

You should also remember that quotes can be used in a string provided they are not the same as those around the string:

var answer = "It's ok";   // A single quote used within double quotes

var answer = "He is called 'Billy'";   // Single quotes used within double quotes

var answer = 'He is called "Billy"';   // Double quotes used within single quotes

We will talk more about strings later in the book.

The next few points are just an overview of what we will cover more of later in the book but, for now, they are included here because they are related to data types.

Numbers

JavaScript contains just one number type and the numbers may or may not have decimal places, for example:

var x1 = 56.00;   // with a decimal place
var x2 = 56;   // without a decimal place

To write very large or very small numbers, you must use an exponential or scientific notation:

var y = 234e5;   // 23400000
var z = 234e-5;   // 0.00234

JavaScript Booleans

Booleans have just two values – True or False

var x = true;

var y = false;

<u>Arrays</u>

In JavaScript, an array is enclosed in square brackets and each item is separated by a comma. Look at the next example which is declaring an array with the name of cars and with three items in it, the names of the cars:

var cars = ["Volvo", "Ford", "Mercedes"];

The indexes in an array are what we call zero-based and this means that the first item will start at 0, the second one is 1 and so on. So, for 10 items in one array, you will go from 0 to 9.

<u>Objects</u>

Objects are contained within curly braces and the properties of the objects are written as pairs of name: value, each pair separated by a comma:

var person = {firstName:"Jane", lastName:"Deer", age:45, eyeColor:"green"};

The object in the example is a person with four properties:

- firstName
- lastName
- age
- eyeColor

typeof Operator

The typeof operator is used to find a variable type. Look at these examples:

```
typeof ""           // Returns "string"
typeof "Jane"        // Returns "string"
typeof "Jane Deer"     // Returns "string"
```

Example

```
typeof 1             // Returns "number"
typeof 253           // Returns "number"
typeof 2.53          // Returns "number"
typeof (1)           // Returns "number"
typeof (5 + 8)       // Returns "number"
```

Primitive Data

Primitive data values are simple single values that have no extra properties or methods. The following primitive types can be returned by the typeof operator:

- boolean
- null

- number
- string
- undefined

For example:

```
typeof "Jane"        // Returns "string"
typeof 2.53          // Returns "number"
typeof true          // Returns "boolean"
typeof false         // Returns "boolean"
```

Complex Data

It can also return one of the following complex data types:

- function
- object

For example:

```
typeof [3, 4, 5, 6]       // Returns "object" and not an array
– see below
typeof {name:jane, age:45} // Returns "object"
typeof function myFunc(){}  // Returns "function"
```

The typeof operator will return "object" because arrays are objects in JavaScript.

Undefined

As we said earlier, a variable that has no value is given the value of undefined. The typeof operator is undefined too:

In JavaScript, a variable without a value has the value undefined. The typeof is also undefined.

var person;   // the value is undefined, the type is undefined

You can empty a variable of its assigned value by setting it to undefined value; the type is also undefined:

person = undefined;   // the value is undefined, the type is undefined

Empty Values

Empty values are not to be confused with undefined values. Empty string variables have both value and type, for example:

var car = "";   // The value is "", the typeof is "string"

Null

Null is nothing in JavaScript, in short, something that is not in existence. Unfortunately, null has a data type of object and you could consider this a kind of bug because typeof null should be null.

Objects can be emptied by setting them to null, like this:

var person = null;   // the value is null, but the type remains an object

You can also empty objects by setting them to undefined:

var person = undefined;   // the value is undefined, the type is undefined

Exercises

Exercise 1:

Create a new variable with a name of carName, assign the value "Ford" to it, and then run it.

<!DOCTYPE html>

<html>

<body>

<p id="demo">Show the result here.</p>

<script>

// Create your variable here

</script>

</body>

</html>

Exercise 2

Create a new variable with a name of number, assign the value 45 to it, and then run it.

```
<!DOCTYPE html>

<html>

<body>


<p id="demo">Show the result here.</p>


<script>

// Create your variable here

</script>


</body>

</html>
```

Type Conversion

It is possible to convert a variable to a new variable with a new data type and we do this by using functions or methods.

Converting a number to a string

To convert a number to a string we use the global method called string() and you can use this on any expression, number, variable or literals. For example:

String(x)   // will return a string from a number variable called x
String(456)   // will return a string from a number literal called 456
String(95 + 28)   // will return a string from a number that is an expression

We can also do the same thing using the number method called toString(), for example:

x.toString()
(456).toString()
(95 + 28).toString()

These ae the methods along with a description of what they do:

Method	Description
toExponential()	Will return a string with a rounded number and written with an exponential notation
toFixed()	Will return a string with rounded number and written using the number of decimal places specified
toPrecision()	Will return a string with a written number of a specified length

Converting a Boolean to a String

To convert a boolean to a string we use the global method called String(), like this:

```
String(false)    // returns "false"
String(true)     // returns "true"
```

We can also use the boolean method called toString() to achieve the same result:

```
false.toString()   // returns "false"
true.toString()    // returns "true"
```

Converting a Date to a String

String() method is also used to convert a date to a string:

String(Date())   // returns "Fri May 17 2017 15:40:19 GMT+0200 (E. Europe Daylight Time)"

And the date method, called toString() will also produce the same result:

Date().toString()   // returns "Fri May 17 2017 15:40:19 GMT+0200 (E. Europe Daylight Time)"

The following are date methods with their descriptions:

Method	Description
getDate()	Gets the day as a number between 1 and 31
getDay()	Gets the weekday as a number between 0 and 6
getFullYear()	Gets the year as a four-digit year - yyyy
getHours()	Gets the hour as a number between 0 and 23
getMilliseconds()	Gets the milliseconds as a number between 0 and 999
getMinutes()	Gets the minutes as a number between 0 and 59

getMonth() between 0 and 11	Gets the month as a number
getSeconds() between 0 and 59	Gets the seconds as a number
getTime() from 1st January 1970	Gets the time in milliseconds

Converting a String to a Number

To convert a string to a number we use the global method called Number(). If a string contains a number like "2.56", it will be converted to a number like 2.56. An empty string will convert to 0 while anything else will convert to NaN – Not a Number.

```
Number("2.56")   // will return as 2.56
Number(" ")     // will return as 0
Number("")      // will return as 0
Number("77 66")  // will return as NaN
```

These are the number methods and what they do:

Method	Description
parseFloat()	will parse a string and return a floating point number
parseInt()	will parse a string and return an integer

The Unary + Operator

This operator is used when we want to convert a variable into a number, for example:

var y = "4";   // y is a string
var x = + y;   // x is a number

If it is not possible to convert the variable, it will still be a number but will have a value of NaN. For example:

var y = "Jane"; // y is a string
var x = + y;   // x is a number (NaN)

Converting a Boolean to a Number

To convert Booleans to numbers we use the global method called Number():

Number(false)   // returns 0
Number(true)   // returns 1

Converting a Date to a Number:

We use the global method called Number() to convert a date into a number, like this:

d = new Date();
Number(d)   // returns 1315484207722

The date method getTime() does the same.

```
d = new Date();
d.getTime()       // returns 1315484207722
```

Automatic Type Conversion

If JavaScript were to attempt an operation on a data type that is "wrong", it will try to convert the value into the "right" type. However, the result is not always going to be what you expect:

```
4 + null   // will return 4        this is because null gets
converted to 0
"4" + null  // will return "4null"   this is because null gets
converted to "null"
"4" + 1    // will return 41        this is because 1 gets
converted to "1"
"4" - 1   // will return 3         this is because "4" gets
converted to 4
"4" * "1"  // will return 4         this is because "4" and "1"
are converted to 4 and 1
```

Automatic String Conversion

When you attempt to "output" a variable or object, JavaScript will automatically call the variable function named toString():

```
document.getElementById("demo").innerHTML = myVar;
```

```
// if myVar = {name:"Gjane"} // toString converts to
"[object Object]"
// if myVar = [4, 5, 6, 7]     // toString converts to "4, 5, 6, 7"
// if myVar = new Date()     // toString converts to "Fri May
18 2017 09:6:55 GMT+0200"
```

You may also convert Booleans and numbers but these are not so visible:

```
// if myVar = 456        // toString converts to "456"
// if myVar = true       // toString converts to "true"
// if myVar = false      // toString converts to "false"
```

Type Conversions

The following shows you what the results are of converting different values in JavaScript to Number, to String and to Boolean:

Original Value		Number	String
Boolean			
""		0	""
	false		
"20"		20	"20"
	true		
"twenty"		NaN	"twenty"
	true		
[ ]		0	""
	true		

[20]	20	"20"
true		
[10,20]	NaN	"10,20"
true		
["twenty"]	NaN	"twenty"
true		
["ten","twenty"]	NaN	"ten,twenty"
true		
"0"	0	"0"
true		
"000"	0	"000"
true		
"1"	1	"1"
true		
0	0	"0"
false		
1	1	"1"
true		
false	0	"false"
false		
function(){}	NaN	
"function(){}"	true	
{}	NaN	"[object

Value	Number	String	Boolean
Object]"			true
null	0	"null"	false
Infinity	Infinity	"Infinity"	true
-Infinity	-Infinity	"-Infinity"	true
NaN	NaN	"Nan"	false
true	1	"true"	true
undefined	NaN	"undefined"	false

The values that are inside the quote marks are strings

Operators

Earlier, I mentioned the assignment operator but there are many more besides. Rather than go into reams of explanations, it is far easier to show you what each operator does:

Arithmetic Operators

JavaScript contains several arithmetic operators and these are used, as you would expect, to carry out arithmetic on numbers:

Operator	Description
+	addition
–	subtraction
*	multiplication
/	division
%	modulus
++	increment
--	decrement

Arithmetic Operations

Typically, an arithmetic operation is done on two numbers, both of which may be literals:

var x = 95 + 55;

or they may be variables:

var x = a + b;

or even expressions:

var x = (95 + 55) * a;

Operators and Operands

The numbers that are inside the arithmetic operation are known as operands while the operation that is being performed between the operands must be defined by the operator:

Operand	Operator	Operand
95	+	55

The addition (+) operator is used to add two numbers:

var x = 4;

var y = 1;

var z = x + y;

The subtraction (-) operator is used to subtract one number from another:

var x = 4;

var y = 1;

var z = x - y;

The multiplication (*) operator is used to multiply one number by another:

var x = 4;

var y = 1;

var z = x * y;

The division (/) operator is used to divide two numbers

var x = 4;

var y = 1;

var z = x / y;

The modular (%) operator is used to return the remainder from division

var x = 4;

var y = 1;

var z = x % y;

The increment (++) operator is used to increment numbers

var x = 4;

x++;

var z = x;

The decrement (--) operator is used to decrement numbers

var x = 4;

x--;

var z = x;

Operator Precedence

Operator precedence is very important and it determines the order operations will be performed in an expression. For example:

var x = 95 + 55 * 3;

So, what is the result here? Is the addition or multiplication carried out first? The answer is the same as it was in school mathematics – the multiplication is always carried out first.

Division and multiplication are top of the precedence order, always done before subtraction and addition. You can change the order of precedence through the use of parentheses:

var x = (95 + 55) * 3;

When we use a set of parentheses, the arithmetic operation inside them is the first to be computed. If an operation uses operators of the same precedence, such as multiplication and division or addition and subtraction, they are worked on from left to right:

var x = 95 + 55 - 3;

Exercises

Exercise 3:

Show the sum of 15 + 5, using two variables called x and y.

```
<!DOCTYPE html>

<html>

<body>


<p id="demo">Show the result here.</p>


<script>

var x;

var y;

</script>


</body>

</html>
```

Exercise 4:

Show the product of 5 * 10, using two variables called x and y.

<!DOCTYPE html>

<html>

<body>

<p id="demo">Show the result here.</p>

<script>

var x;

var y;

</script>

</body>

</html>

Assignment Operators

The assignment operators are what we use to assign values to variables:

Operator as	Example	Same
=	x = y	x = y
+=	x += y	x = x + y
-=	x -= y	x = x − y
*=	x * = y	x = x * y
/=	x / = y	x = x / y
%=	x % = y	x = x % y

The addition assignment (+=) operator is used to add values to variables:

var x = 15;
x += 5;

The subtraction assignment (-=) is used to subtract values form variables:

var x = 15;
x -= 5;

The multiplication assignment (*=) operator is used to multiply variables:

```
var x = 15;
x *= 5;
```

The division assignment (/=) operator is used to divide variables:

```
var x = 15;
x /= 5;
```

The modular assignment (%=) operator is used to assign remainders to variables:

```
var x = 15;
x %= 5;
```

Exercises

Exercise 5:

Using the += operator, add the value of 5 to the variable called x

<!DOCTYPE html>

<html>

<body>

<p id="demo"></p>

<script>

var x = 10;

// **add your code in here**

document.getElementById("demo").innerHTML = x;

</script>

</body>

</html>

Exercise 6:

Using the -= operator, subtract the value of 5 from the variable called x.

```
<!DOCTYPE html>

<html>

<body>


<p id="demo"></p>


<script>

var x = 10;
```

// add your code in here

```
document.getElementById("demo").innerHTML = x;

</script>


</body>
</html>
```

String Operators

String operators are used to perform operations on strings:

We can use the + operator to concatenate or add two strings together. For example:

txt1 = "Jane";

txt2 = "Deer";

txt3 = txt1 + " " + txt2;

txt3 will output a result of:

Jane Deer

We can use the += operator to add strings together as well:

txt1 = "What a wonderful ";

txt1 += "sunny day";

txt1 will output a result of:

What a wonderful sunny day

Although this is called the addition assignment operator, when we use the + operator on a string it is named a concatenation operator.

Adding Strings and Numbers

If you add two numbers together, the output is the sum of those numbers but, if you add a string and a number, the output is a string:

x = 5 + 10;
y = "5" + 10;
z = "Hello" + 10;
The output will be:

15

510

Hello10

Comparison and Logical Operators

We use these operators to test to see if a condition or statement is true or false, i.e. to see if there is any equality or any difference between values or variables.

Comparison Operators

Supposing that x = 5, the list below explains the comparison operators:

Operator	Description		
		Comparing	Returns

==	equal to	x == 8
	false	
x == 5	true	
x == "5"	true	
===	equal value and equal type	x ===
5	true	
x === "5"	false	
!=	not equal	x != 8
	true	
!==	not equal value or not equal type	x !==
5	false	
x !== "5"	true	
x !== 8	true	
>	greater than	x > 8
	false	
<	less than	x < 8
	true	
>=	greater than or equal to	x >= 8
	false	

<=	less than or equal to	x <= 8 true

How Comparison Operators are Used

A comparison operator is used in a conditional statement for the purpose of comparing values and then taking the right action as per the result:

if (age < 18) text = "Not old enough";

Logical Operators

We use logical operators to determine what logic there is between values or variables. Supposing that x = 6 and y = 3, this next list explains logical operators:

Operator	Description	Example
&&	and	(x < 10 && y > 1) is true
||	or	(x == 5 || y == 5) is false
!	not	!(x == y) is true

Conditional or Ternary Operator

There is also a conditional operator in JavaScript that is used to assign values to variables based on specific conditions and the syntax used is:

variablename = (condition) ? value1:value2

For example:

var voteable = (age < 18) ? "Not old enough":"Old enough";

Yourself »

If the variable called age holds a value that is lower than 18, variable voteable will output a result of "Not old enough". If it is above 18, the output will be "old enough"

Comparing Different Types

When you compare sets of data that are of different types, you might get a result you did not expect. For example, if you compare a string and a number, JavaScript converts that string into a number, while an empty string will convert to 0 and non-numeric strings will convert to Nan, and this is always false.

Case	Value
4 < 24	true
4 < "24"	true

4 < "Jane"   false

4 > "Jane"   false

4 == "Jane"   false

"4" < "24"   false

"4" > "24"   true

"4" == "24"   false

When we compare two strings, "4" is greater than "24" because, in alphabetical terms, 2 is less than 4. To make sure you get the right result, you should always convert the variable to the correct type before you carry out the comparison:

```javascript
age = Number(age);

if (isNaN(age)) {

    voteable = "The input isn't a number";

} else {

    voteable = (age < 18) ? "Not old enough" : "Old enough";

}
```

Exercises

Exercise 7:

Which is the right comparison operator to show "true", when:

4 is less than 8?

<!DOCTYPE html>

<html>

<body>

<p id="demo">Show the result here.</p>

<script>

document.getElementById("demo").innerHTML = 4 8;

</script>

</body>

</html>

Exercise 8:

Which is the right the correct comparison operator to show "true", when:

12 is NOT equal to 6?

```
<!DOCTYPE html>

<html>

<body>


<p id="demo">Show the result here.</p>


<script>

document.getElementById("demo").innerHTML = 12 6;

</script>


</body>

</html>
```

If / else Statements

These are classed as conditional statements that perform a specific action depending on the conditions in the statement. Sometimes, you are going to want your code to do something depending on a decision and this is where you use the conditional statements. JavaScript has these:

- **if** – used to specify code blocks that are only to be executed if a certain condition evaluates true
- **else** – used to specify code blocks that are only to be executed if the same condition evaluates false
- **else if** – used to specify a new condition that needs testing, only if the first condition evaluates to false
- **switch** – used for specifying several alternative code blocks to be executed.

The if Statement

The if statement is used when you have a block of code you want to execute if a specified condition evaluates true. This is the syntax:

```
if (condition) {
    code block for executing if the condition evaluates true
}
```

Note that if is always in lowercase – if you use If or IF, you will get an error. Here is an example for you to have a go at:

Create a greeting that says "Hello" if it is before 18:00:

```
if (hour < 18) {
    greeting = "Hello";
}
```

The output will be:

Hello

The else Statement

The else statement is to be used when you want to specify a code block for executing only if the specified condition evaluates false. The syntax is:

```
if (condition) {
    code block that is executed if the condition evaluates true
} else {
    code block to be executed if the condition evaluates false
}
```

Another example for you to try:

Create a greeting that says "Hello" if it is before 18:00 and says, "Good evening" if it is later:

```
if (hour < 18) {
    greeting = "Hello";
} else {
    greeting = "Good evening";
}
```

The output will be:

Good day

<u>The else if Statement</u>

The else if statement is to be used when you want to specify another statement if the first condition evaluates false. The syntax used is:

```
if (condition1) {
    code block to be executed if condition1 evaluates true
} else if (condition2) {
    code block to be executed if conditon1 evaluates false and
condition2 evaluates true
} else {
    code block to be executed if both condition1 and
condition2 evaluate to false
}
```

For example:

Create a greeting that says "Good Morning" if the time is before 10:00 AM, or, if between 10:00 and 20:00, it says "Hello" or, if later than 20:00 it says, "Good Evening":

```
if (time < 10) {
    greeting = "Good Morning";
} else if (time < 20) {
    greeting = "Hello";
} else {
    greeting = "Good Evening";
}
```

The output will be:

Good day

Exercises

Exercise 9

Using the if statement, output the text "Great Job!" if 4 is greater than 3

```
<!DOCTYPE html>

<html>

<body>


<p id="demo"></p>


<script>
if () {

    document.getElementById("demo").innerHTML = "Great Job!";

}
</script>


</body>
```

</html>

Exercise 10

Change the value assigned to variable firstName to ensure the if statement will run

```
<!DOCTYPE html>

<html>

<body>


<p id="demo"></p>


<script>

var firstName = "George";


if (firstName === "Jane") {

    document.getElementById("demo").innerHTML = "Hello Jane!";

}

</script>


</body>

</html>
```

Boolean Logic and Switch Statements

Boolean Values

Booleans can only return one of two values – True or False – and often this is the data type that you will need in your programs.

The Boolean() Function

The Boolean() function is used to determine if a variable or expression is true. For example:

Boolean(12 > 7)   // will return true

Or:

(12 > 7)   // will also return true
12 > 7   // will also return true

Comparisons and Conditions

We have already covered comparison operators and of conditional statements in earlier sections but, just as a refresher, here are a few examples:

Operator Example	Description	
== == "Tuesday")	equal to	if (day
> (earnings > 9000)	greater than	if
< < 18)	less than	if (age

Boolean values of expressions are fundamental to conditions and comparisons in JavaScript.

Everything That has a "Real" Value is True

Examples

95

3.14

-17

"Good Day"

"false"

6 + 3 + 3.14

4 < 7

Everything That Doesn't Have a "Real" is False

0 evaluates false in Boolean:

var x = 0;
Boolean(x);   // returns false

As does the value of -0:

var x = -0;
Boolean(x);   // returns false

And the value of "", which is an empty string:

var x = "";
Boolean(x);   // returns false

Also false is the value of undefined:

var x;
Boolean(x);   // returns false

And the value of null:

var x = null;
Boolean(x);   // returns false

As is the value of false:

```
var x = false;
Boolean(x);      // returns false
```

And the value of NaN:

```
var x = 10 / "H";
Boolean(x);      // returns false
```

Booleans Can be Objects

Usually, a Boolean is a primitive value that has been created from a literal:

```
var x = false;
```

but a Boolean may also be defined as an object by using the keyword new, for example:

new: var y = new Boolean (False)

Have a look at this

```
var x = false;
var y = new Boolean(false);

// typeof x will return Boolean
// typeof y will return object
```

NOTE – don't go creating Boolean objects because it will slow down the speed the code executes at.

Use of the new keyword makes things a little complicated and you may get some odd results:

When you use the ==operator, equal Booleans evaluate equal:

var x = false;
var y = new Boolean(false);

// (x == y) is true as both x and y have got equal values

When you use the === operator, equal Booleans will not be equal because this operator wants equality in the type and in the value.

var x = false;
var y = new Boolean(false);

// (x === y) is false as both x and y have got different types

Even worse, objects can't be compared:

var x = new Boolean(false);
var y = new Boolean(false);

// (x == y) is false as objects can't be compared

Note that there is a difference between (x===y) and (x==y).

The Switch Statement

Switch statements are used when we want to carry out differing actions depending on differing conditions, i.e. to choose from one of several code blocks to execute. The syntax is:

```
switch(expression) {
    case n:
        code block
        break;
    case n:
        code block
        break;
    default:
        code block
}
```

This is how the switch statement works:

- The expression value is compared against each case value
- If a match occurs, the block of code associated with the match will be executed.

For example:

The method called getMonth() will return the month represented as a number from 0 to 11, i.e. January=0, February=1, etc.

In this example, we are using the number of the month to calculate the name of the month:

```
var month;
switch (new Date().getMonth()) {
    case 0:
      month = "January";
      break;
    case 1:
      month = "February";
      break;
    case 2:
      month = "March";
      break;
    case 3:
      month = "April";
      break;
    case 4:
      month = "May";
      break;
    case 5:
      month = "June";
      break;
```

```
case 6:
   month = "July";

   break;

case 7:

   month = "August";
   break;

case 8:

   month = "September";
   break;

case 9:

   month = "October";
   break;

case 10:

   month = "November";
    break;

case 11:

   month = "December";
}
```

The Break Keyword

Notice the use of the break keyword in the above example. Whenever JavaScript comes to this keyword, it will break out of the switch block. This results in the program halting the execution of any more code until the case inside the block has been tested. When a match occurs, a break happens and no more testing is needed.

Using a break can save you a lot of time in executing code because it will skip over all of the code in the switch block once the match has been found. One thing to note, you don't need to put a break after the final case in the block because the block will end at this point anyway.

The Default Keyword

The default keyword is used when you want to specify what code is to run if no match occurs.

The getDay() method is used to return a weekday as a number from 0 to 6.

Write a default message if today isn't Monday (1) or Tuesday (2):

```
switch (new Date().getDay()) {
    case 1:
        text = "Today is Monday";
```

```
      break;
   case 2:
      text = "Today is Tuesday";
      break;
   default:
      text = "I can't wait for Friday!";
}
```

It isn't necessary for the default to be the last case in the switch block:

```
switch (new Date().getDay()) {
   default:
      text = "I can't wait for Friday!";
      break;
   case 1:
      text = "Today is Monday";
      break;
   case 2:
      text = "Today is Tuesday";
}
```

However, if you do not have the default as the final case in the statement, you must not forget to finish the default case using a break statement

Common Code Blocks

On occasion, you are going to need different switch cases for one piece of code. In the next example, case 3 and 4 share one code block and 6 and 0 share another:

Example

```
switch (new Date().getDay()) {
    case 3:
    case 4:
        text = "Soon it will be the weekend";
        break;
    case 0:
    case 6:
        text = "The weekend is here!";
        break;
    default:
        text = "Can't wait for the weekend!";
}
```

Exercises

Exercise 11

The following switch statement has not got a default case so add it in at the bottom of the switch and set the text to say, "That is a strange fruit!"

<!DOCTYPE html>

<html>

<body>

<input id="myInput" type="text" value="Tutti Frutti">

<button onclick="checkFruit()">Check Fruit</button>

<p id="demo"></p>

<script>

function checkFruit() {

  var text;

  var fruits = document.getElementById("myInput").value;

```
switch(fruits) {

  case "Apple":

    text = "Apples are good!";

    break;

  case "Banana":

    text = "I don't like Banana.";

    break;

  case "Satsuma":

    text = "Such a juicy Satsuma!";

    break;

  // this is where the default goes

}

document.getElementById("demo").innerHTML = text;

}
```

</script>

Exercise 12

Finish this switch statement by adding in cases for Mercedes, Volvo, and Citroen. The variable value text should be set to

"German car" for Mercedes, "Swedish car" for Volvo and "French car" for Citroen. Also, you need to add a default case where it says, "Unknown car name".

```
<!DOCTYPE html>

<html>

<body>


<input id="myInput" type="text" value="BMW">

<button onclick="checkCar()">Check Car</button>

<p id="demo"></p>


<script>

function checkCar() {

  var text;

  var favCar = document.getElementById("myInput").value;


  switch(favCar) {

    // your code goes here
```

```
    }

    document.getElementById("demo").innerHTML = text;

}

</script>


</body>

</html>
```

Functions

JavaScript functions are blocks of code that are designed to carry out specific tasks. It will be executed when it is invoked or called. For example:

```
function myFunction(p1, p2) {
    return p1 * p2;        // This function will return the
product of p1 and p2
}
```

Function Syntax

We define the function using the function keyword, then the name and then a set of parentheses. When you name a function, you follow the same rules as those for a variable:

- You can use letters a to z or A to Z, numbers 0 to 9, $ and _ in the name

The pair of parentheses can have names of parameters and, if more than one, each must be separated by a comma, i.e. (parameter1, parameter2, ...)

The code that is the function executes goes inside a set of curly brackets – {}:

```
function name(parameter1, parameter2, parameter3) {
    code that is going to be executed
}
```

The function parameters are those names that are listed within the function definition and the function arguments are real values that the function receives when it is called or invoked. Within the function, the parameters act like local variables.

Function Invocation

As I said, the code that is in the function executes when it is called, for example when something happens, like a user pressing a button. Or it may be called by the code itself or be self-invoked

Function Return

When JavaScript gets to a return statement, the function ceases to execute. However, if the function had been invoked via a return statement, it will go back and continue executing that code after the invoking statement. Functions can often compute return values and that return value will go back to the caller. For example:

Calculate the product from two numbers, and then return the result:

```
var x = myFunction(5, 4);      // The function is called and
the return value goes to x
```

```
function myFunction(a, b) {
    return a * b;              // The function will return the
product of a and b
}
```

The value of x will be:

20

Why Functions?

Simply because, once you have defined the code, you can reuse it as many times as you want. Use it with any number of different arguments and each will produce a different result:

Convert Fahrenheit to Celsius:

```
function toCelsius(fahrenheit) {
    return (5/9) * (fahrenheit-32);
}
document.getElementById("demo").innerHTML =
toCelsius(77);
```

If you look at the example above, you will note that we used the () operator to invoke the function. toCelcius() is referring to the function object and toCelcius() refers to the result from the function. If you try to access a function without using the () operator, you will get the definition and not the result of the function:

For example:

```
function toCelsius(fahrenheit) {
    return (5/9) * (fahrenheit-32);
}
document.getElementById("demo").innerHTML =
toCelsius;
```

Functions Used as Variable Values

You can use functions in the same way that you use variables, in all different calculations, formulas and assignments.

For example:

Rather than a variable to store the functions' return value:

```
var x = toCelsius(77);
var text = "The temperature is " + x + " Celsius";
```

You can just use the function as a value of a variable:

```
var text = "The temperature is " + toCelsius(77) + " Celsius";
```

Exercises

Exercise 13

Call the function in this code:

```
<!DOCTYPE html>

<html>

<body>


<p id="demo"></p>


<script>

function myFunction() {

    document.getElementById("demo").innerHTML = "Hi
Guys!";

}

// this is where the function is called

</script>


</body>
```

</html>

Exercise 14

Use the function to show the value of 10 * 10:

<!DOCTYPE html>

<html>

<body>

<p id="demo"></p>

<script>

function myFunction() {

   // your code goes here

}

document.getElementById("demo").innerHTML = myFunction();

</script>

</body>

</html>

Arrays

Arrays are special kinds of variables, able to hold several values at any one time. If you have a whole list of items, such as car names, to store them in one variable would look something like this:

var car1 = "Ford";
var car2 = "Mercedes";
var car3 = "Volvo";

However, if you wanted to loop through these cars to find a particular one, and you had 30 cars, not 3 of them, you would use an array. An array will hold all of the values in one name and you can get access to them by using the index number.

Creating an Array

The easiest way to create an array is to use an array literal. The syntax is:

var array_name = [item1, item2, ...];

An example:

var cars = ["Ford", "Mercedes", "Volvo"];

Each declaration can go over several lines and line breaks and spaces are not important:

```
var cars = [
    "Ford",
    "Mercedes",
    "Volvo"
];
```

Note the comma the end of each element except for the final one – the final comma is not consistent across all browsers and, for example, if you did it in IE8, you would find it fails

Using the Keyword new

In the next example, we have created an array and we have assigned values to it:

```
var cars = new Array("Ford", "Mercedes", "Volvo");
```

Both of the above examples are identical in what result they produce. You really don't need to use the keyword new; to keep things simple, stick to using the first example, the array literal.

Accessing the Array Elements

Each array element is referred to by the index number. The following statement will access the value of the first element that is in the array called cars:

var name = cars[0];

The next statement modifies that first element:

cars[0] = "Audi";

For example:

var cars = ["Audi", "Mercedes", "Volvo"];
document.getElementById("demo").innerHTML = cars[0];

Array elements arc zero-indexed and the first one is indexed [0], the second indexed [1] and so on.

Accessing the Full Array

To access the full array in JavaScript, we use the name of the array, for example:

var cars = ["Audi", "Mercedes", "Volvo"];
document.getElementById("demo").innerHTML = cars;

Arrays are Objects

Arrays are also special object types and, using the typeof operator will return a type of object for any array. However, it is best to refer to them as arrays and each array will access its elements by using numbers. In the next example, person [0] will return Jane:

var person = ["Jane", "Deer", 45];

whereas in an object, names are used to get access to the members of the object. In the next example, person.firstName will return Jane:

var person = {firstName:"Jane", lastName:"Deer", age:45};

Array Elements Can Be Objects

Variables may be objects as well and, as we know, an array is a special type of object. Because of this, each array can hold different types of variables. For example, you can have functions, objects and even arrays in the same array:

myArray[0] = Date.now;
myArray[1] = myFunction;
myArray[2] = myCars;

Array Properties and Methods

The real strength of the array comes from the methods and properties that are built in, for example:

var x = cars.length;   // The property called length will return the number of array elements
var y = cars.sort();   // The method called sort() will sort the arrays

We will be looking at array methods in more detail shortly.

The Length Property

The length property will return the array length or the number of elements in the array.

For example

var fruits = ["Apple", "Banana", "Orange", "Pineapple"];
fruits.length;   // the length of fruits is 4

The length property will always be one higher than the highest index in the array:

<u>Looping Array Elements</u>

If you want to loop through an array, the best way is to use a for loop. For example:

var fruits, text, fLen, i;

fruits = ["Apple", "Banana", "Orange", "Pineapple"];
fLen = fruits.length;
text = "<ul>";
for (i = 0; i < fLen; i++) {
   text += "<li>" + fruits[i] + "</li>";
}

<u>Adding Array Elements</u>

The best way to add new elements into an array is to use the push method, like this:

```
var fruits = ["Apple", "Banana", "Orange", "Pineapple"];
fruits.push("Kiwi");          // this adds a new element,
called Kiwi, to the array
```

You can also do this by using the length property:

```
var fruits = ["Apple", "Banana", "Orange", "Pineapple"];
fruits[fruits.length] = "Kiwi";   // this also adds a new
element called kiwi to the array
```

Associative Arrays

Most computer programming languages will support arrays that have named indexes and these are known as associative arrays or hashes. However, JavaScript doesn't support named index arrays but it does support numbered indexes:

```
var person = [];
person[0] = "Jane";
person[1] = "Deer";
person[2] = 45;
var x = person.length;      // person.length returns 3
var y = person[0];          // person[0] returns "Jane"
```

Note:

If you try to use named indexes, all JavaScript will do is redefine the array into a standard object and some methods and properties of the array will produce results that are not correct:

```
var person = [];
person["firstName"] = "Jane";
person["lastName"] = "Deer";
person["age"] = 45;
var x = person.length;      // person.length returns 0
var y = person[0];          // person[0] returns undefined
```

Summary

- Arrays always use numbered indexes while objects will use named indexes. An array is a special type of object with numbered instead of named indexes. There is no support for associative arrays in JavaScript.

- If you want the element names as strings or text, use an object; if you want the element names as numbers, use arrays.

- Avoid the use of new Array(); there is no need to use it. Instead, use []. Both of the following statements will create a new array called points that is empty:

```
var points = new Array();    // Not recommended
var points = [];             // Recommended
```

While these two statements both create an array that has 6 numbers:

var points = new Array(20, 101, 2, 7, 35, 15); // Not recommended

var points = [20, 101, 2, 7, 35, 15];   // Recommended

Using the new keyword just makes things difficult and can produce results that you don't expect:

var points = new Array(20, 101); // this will create an array that has 2 elements – 20 and 101

If you remove an element:

var points = new Array(20);   // you will get an array with 20 elements that are all undefined

Exercises

Exercise 15

Create an array, call it cars and assign it with the following values: "Ford", "Mercedes" and "Opel", then display it.

<!DOCTYPE html>

<html>

<body>

<p id="demo">The result is displayed here.</p>

<script>

// The array is created here

</script>

</body>

</html>

Exercise 16:

Change the first item of the cars array to read "Volvo" – refer to the index number and then display the entire array

```
<!DOCTYPE html>

<html>

<body>


<p id="demo"></p>


<script>

var cars = ["Ford", "Mercedes", "Opel"];

document.getElementById("demo").innerHTML = cars;

</script>


</body>

</html>
```

JavaScript Array Methods

As I said earlier, the real strength in the array is in the methods.

Converting Arrays to Strings

To convert an array to a string of values, each one separated by commas, we use the toString() method:

var fruits = ["Apple", "Banana", "Orange", "Pineapple"];
document.getElementById("demo").innerHTML = fruits.toString();

You can also use the join() method to join all of the array elements together in a string. It works like toString() but you can also specify which separator to use:

var fruits = ["Apple", "Banana","Orange", "Pineapple"];
document.getElementById("demo").innerHTML = fruits.join(" * ");

Popping and Pushing

When you are working with an array, you can easily add new elements and remove them as well. This is where popping and pushing come in. Popping removes an element, pushing adds an element.

Popping

To take the last element out of an array, we use the pop() method:

var fruits = ["Apple", "Banana", "Orange", "Pineapple"];
fruits.pop();   // takes the last element, Pineapple, out of the array

The result of the pop() method is the value of the element that got popped out:

var fruits = ["Apple", "Banana", "Orange", "Pineapple"];
var x = fruits.pop();   // the value of x is "Pineapple"

Pushing

To add a new element to the end of the array, we use the push() method:

var fruits = ["Apple", "Banana", "Orange", "Pineapple"];
fruits.push("Lime");   // this adds a new element called Lime to the end of the array

The result of the push() method is the new length of the array:

```
var fruits = ["Apple", "Banana", "Orange", "Pineappple"];
var x = fruits.push("Lime");   // the value of x is 5
```

Shifting Elements

Shifting is the same as popping but works on the first array element rather than the last. The shift() method will take the first element out of the array and shift all the others to lower indexes.

```
var fruits = ["Apple", "Banana", "Orange", "Pineapple"];
fruits.shift();        // takes the first element, Apple, out of
the array
```

The result of the shift() method is the string that is shifted out of the array

```
var fruits = ["Apple", "Banana", "Orange", "Pineapple"];
fruits.shift();        // Will return "Apple"
```

On the other hand, the unshift() method puts a new element into the start of the array and then unshifts the older elements:

```
var fruits = ["Apple", "Banana", "Orange", "Pineapple"];
fruits.unshift("Lime");   // will add a new element called
"Lime" to the array
```

The result of the unshift() method is the new length of the array

```
var fruits = ["Apple", "Banana", "Orange", "Pineapple"];
fruits.unshift("Lime");    // will return 5
```

Changing Elements

We access the elements in the array by their index number. Because arrays are zero-indexed, the first element will have an array index of [0[, the second will have an index of [1], the third, an index of [2], and so on.

```
var fruits = ["Apple", "Banana", "Orange", "Pineapple"];
fruits[0] = "Melon";       // will change the first element of
the array to "Melon"
```

One easy way to add a new element to an array is using the length property

```
var fruits = ["Apple", "Banana", "Orange", "Pineapple"];
fruits[fruits.length] = "Melon";       // Will add a new
element called "Melon" to the array
```

Deleting Elements

Because arrays in JavaScript are objects, we use the delete operator to delete an element:

```
var fruits = ["Apple", "Banana", "Orange", "Pineapple"];
delete fruits[0];       // Will change the first element in the
array to undefined
```

However, although you can use the delete operator, you may find yourself with undefined holes in your array so it is better to use the pop() method or the shift() method instead.

Splicing Arrays

To add a new item to the array we can use the splice() method:

var fruits = ["Apple", "Banana", "Orange", "Pineapple"];
fruits.splice(3, 0, "Lime", "Melon");

the first parameter of 3 is defining where in the array the new elements are added, or spliced in while the second one, 0, defines the number of elements to be removed, in this case, none. "Lime" and "Melon" are the new elements that are to be added in

Removing Elements Using splice()

Using some clever setting of parameters, you can remove, or splice, elements from the array without leaving any holes.

var fruits = ["Apple", "Banana", "Orange", "Pineapple"];
fruits.splice(0, 1);   // Will remove the first element in the array

the first parameter of 0 is defining where the new elements are being added in and the second one, 1, is defining the number of elements to be removed. No other parameters are needed because no new elements are being added

Concatenating Arrays

We can create new arrays by merging or concatenating two or more existing arrays using the concat() method. The following example shows you how to merge two existing arrays:

```
var myGirls = ["Celia", "Laurie"];
var myBoys = ["Johnny", "Toby","Larry"];
var myChildren = myGirls.concat(myBoys);    // Concatenates (joins) myGirls and myBoys
```

The concat() method does not change the existing arrays. It always returns a new array.

The concat() method can take any number of array arguments:

Example (Merging Three Arrays)

```
var arr1 = ["Celia", "Laurie"];
var arr2 = ["Johnny", "Toby","Larry"];
var arr3 = ["Richard", "Martin"];
var myChildren = arr1.concat(arr2, arr3);    // this will concatenate or merge arr1 with arr2 and arr3
```

The concat() method is also able to take arguments in the form of values. The next example shows you how to merge arrays with values:

```
var arr1 = ["Celia", "Laurie"];
var myChildren = arr1.concat(["Johnny", "Toby","Larry"]);
```

Slicing Arrays

We can take a piece of one array and put it in a new array using the slice() method. The next example shows how to slice a piece of array beginning at element index 1, in this case, "Banana":

```
var fruits =
["Apple", "Banana", "Lime", "Orange", "Pineapple"];
var citrus = fruits.slice(1);
```

This method will also create new arrays but will not take any elements out of the source array. This example will show you how to slice part of an array out beginning at element 3, "Lime":

```
var fruits =
["Apple", "Banana", "Lime", "Orange", "Pineapple"];
var citrus = fruits.slice(3);
```

The slice() method is able to take two arguments. The method will then choose elements from the first argument up to, not including, the last argument. For example:

var fruits =

["Apple", "Banana", "Lime", "Orange", "Pineapple"];

var citrus = fruits.slice(1, 3);

If the final argument is left out, as in the first couple of examples, the slice() method will slice the remainder of the array out.

var fruits =

["Apple", "Banana", "Lime", "Orange", "Pineapple"];

var citrus = fruits.slice(2);

Automatic toString()

When a primitive value is expected as a result, JavaScript will convert an array to a string that is comma-separated automatically. This will always happen when you attempt to output arrays. Both of these next examples will output the exact same result:

Example 1

var fruits = ["Apple", "Banana", "Orange", "Pineapple"];
document.getElementById("demo").innerHTML = fruits.toString();

Example 2

var fruits = ["Apple", "Banana", "Orange", "Pineapple"];
document.getElementById("demo").innerHTML = fruits;

Note – every JavaScript object has a toString() method

Exercises

Exercise 17:

Using the pop() method, remove the last item that is in the fruits array.

```
<!DOCTYPE html>

<html>

<body>


<p id="demo"></p>


<script>

var fruits = ["Apple", "Banana", "Orange"];

document.getElementById("demo").innerHTML = fruits;

</script>


</body>

</html>
```

Exercise 18

Using the push() method, add a new item into fruits:
Pineapple

<!DOCTYPE html>

<html>

<body>

<p id="demo"></p>

<script>

var fruits = ["Apple", "Banana", "Orange"];

document.getElementById("demo").innerHTML = fruits;

</script>

</body>

</html>

Sorting Arrays

The JavaScript sort() method is the strongest of all the array methods.

Sorting an Array

To sort an array into alphabetical order, we use the sort() method:

var fruits = ["Orange", "Apple", "Pineapple", "Banana"];
fruits.sort();   // this sorts the array elements into alphabetical order

Reversing an Array

To reverse the array elements, we use the reverse() method to sort into descending order:

var fruits = ["Orange", "Apple", "Pineapple", "Banana"];
fruits.sort();   // Will sort the array elements
fruits.reverse();   // Will reverse the order of the array elements

Numeric Sort

The sort() function will sort values as strings by default. While this works good for strings, it won't work so well when you sort numbers as strings. If you tried to sort 35 and 101 into order, 35 would be bigger than 101 because 3 is bigger than 1. If you try to sort numbers using the sort() method, you will get the wrong results so, to fix this, we use a compare function:

```
var points = [20, 102, 2, 7, 35, 14];
points.sort(function(a, b){return a - b});
```

And the same way can be used for sorting into descending order:

```
var points = [20, 102, 2, 7, 35, 14];
points.sort(function(a, b){return b - a});
```

The Compare Function

The compare function is used to define other sorting orders. It should return either a positive, zero or negative value, depending on what the arguments are:

```
function(a, b){return a-b}
```

When two values are compared using the sort() function, the values are sent to the compare function and sorted according to the returned value – negative, positive or zero. For example:

- When 35 and 101 are compared, the sort() method will call the compare function (35, 101)

- The compare function will calculate 35-101 and return a negative value of -66
- The sort() function sorts value 35 as being lower than value 101

This piece of code can be used to play around with alphabetical and numerical sorting:

```
<button onclick="myFunction1()">Sort
Alphabetically</button>
<button onclick="myFunction2()">Sort
Numerically</button>

<p id="demo"></p>

<script>
var points = [20, 102, 2, 7, 35, 14];
document.getElementById("demo").innerHTML = points;

function myFunction1() {
  points.sort();
  document.getElementById("demo").innerHTML = points;
}
function myFunction2() {
  points.sort(function(a, b){return a - b});
  document.getElementById("demo").innerHTML = points;
```

```
}
</script>
```

Sorting Arrays in Random Order

An example:

```
var points = [20, 102, 2, 7, 35, 14];
points.sort(function(a, b){return 0.5 - Math.random()});
```

Finding the Highest or Lowest Values

To find the highest array value:

```
var points = [20, 102, 2, 7, 35, 14];
points.sort(function(a, b){return b - a});
// now points[0] will contain the highest value
```

To find the lowest array value:

```
var points = [20, 102, 2, 7, 35, 14];
points.sort(function(a, b){return a - b});
// now points[0] will contain the lowest value
```

Sorting Object Arrays

Arrays in JavaScript will often contain objects:

```
var cars = [
{type:"Mercedes", year:2015},
{type:"Volvo", year:2003},
{type:"Audi", year:2011}];
```

Even if the objects have properties that are of different types of data, we can still use the sort() method. To do this, we write a compare function that we use to compare the values of the properties:

```
cars.sort(function(a, b){return a.year - b.year});
```

However, comparing the string properties is not quite so straightforward:

```
cars.sort(function(a, b){
   var x = a.type.toLowerCase();
   var y = b.type.toLowerCase();
   if (x < y) {return -1;}
   if (x > y) {return 1;}
   return 0;
});
```

Properties and Objects

The most important bit of any object in Javascript are the properties

Properties

These are the values that are associated with an object, which is, in turn, a collection of properties that are not ordered. Properties may be changed, deleted or added but some properties will be read-only.

Accessing Properties

To access an object property, we use the following syntax:

objectName.property   // person.age

or

objectName["property"]   // person["age"]

or

objectName[expression]   // x = "age"; person[x]

The expression has go to evaluate to the name of a property. Have a look at the following examples:

Example 1

person.firstname + " is " + person.age + " years old.";

Example 2

person["firstname"] + " is " + person["age"] + " years old.";

for...in Loop

The for...in statement is used to loop through object properties and the syntax we use is:

```
for (the variable in the object) {
    the code that is to be executed
}
```

The code that is inside the for...in loop is executed once for each of the properties. To loop through the object properties:

```
var person = {fname:"Jane", lname:"Deer", age:22};

for (x in person) {
    txt += person[x];
}
```

Adding A New Property

New properties can be added to existing objects very easily; all you do is provide it with a value. Let's assume that the object called person is already in existence so you can easily give it some new properties:

person.nationality = "French";

The naming rules for JavaScript apply to naming methods or properties and you may not use any of the reserved keywords for this purpose.

Deleting A Property

To delete properties from objects we use the delete keyword:

```
var person = {firstName:"Jane", lastName:"Deer", age:45,
eyeColor:"Green"};
delete person.age;   // or delete person["age"];
```

The delete keyword will remove the property and the value of the property. After it has been deleted, you must add the property back in before you can use it again.

The delete operator is specially designed for properties of objects and has no effect whatsoever on functions or variables. However, you may not use the delete operator on any predefined properties of objects as your application will crash.

Property Attributes

Every property has a name and a value, the latter of which is an attribute of the property. The other attributes are writable, configurable and enumerable. Each of these attributes will define access to the property, i.e. is it writable, or readable? All JavaScript attuites may be read but the only that can be changed is the value attribute and that is only if it is a writable property.

Prototype Properties

All JavaScript objects will inherit properties from their prototype. You cannot use the delete keyword to delete an inherited property but deleting the prototype will have an effect on all of the objects that were inherited from that prototype.

Objects and Methods

Methods are the actions that objects can have performed on them and they are properties with function definitions.

Property	Value
firstName	Jane
lastName	Deer
age	45
eyeColor	green
fullName	function() {return this.firstName + " " + this.lastName;}

Methods are also functions that are stored as properties of objects.

Accessing the Object Methods

We use the following syntax to create object methods:

methodName : function() { lines of code }

And the following syntax is used to access the object method:

objectName.methodName()

Usually, fullName() will be described as a method of the object called person and fullName as the property. This property executes as a function when we use () to invoke it. This next example shows you how to access the fullName() method of the person object:

name = person.fullName();

If you don't use () when you access fullName, you will get the function definition returned instead.

Using the Built-In Methods

There are several built-in methods in JavaScript and this one shows you how to convert text to uppercase using the toUpperCase() method of String:

var message = "Hi Guys!";
var x = message.toUpperCase();

When the code is executed, the value will be printed in uppercase letters – HI GUYS!

Adding a New Method

To add a new method to an object we use the constructor function:

```
function person(firstName, lastName, age, eyeColor) {
    this.firstName = firstName;
    this.lastName = lastName;
    this.age = age;
    this.eyeColor = eyeColor;
    this.changeName = function (name) {
        this.lastName = name;
    };
}
```

the function called changeName() will assign the name value to the lastName property in person

Loops and Iteration

Loops are used to execute a piece of code repeatedly. They are especially good when you want to run one piece of code several times but with a different value each time. This is often going to be the case when you are working with arrays. Instead of inputting this:

```
text += cars[0] + "<br>";
text += cars[1] + "<br>";
text += cars[2] + "<br>";
text += cars[3] + "<br>";
text += cars[4] + "<br>";
text += cars[5] + "<br>";
```

You could just do this:

```
for (i = 0; i < cars.length; i++) {
    text += cars[i] + "<br>";
}
```

Different Loops

JavaScript provides support for several kinds of loop:

- for...loop – will loop through one block of code several times

- for...in loop – will loop through object properties
- do...while loop – will loop through one block of code while a condition evaluates true

The for...loop

This is the loop that you will use most often and use the following syntax:

```
for (statement 1; statement 2; statement 3) {
    the code block being executed
}
```

Statement 1 will be executed before the code block or loop starts

Statement 2 will define the condition required for the loop to run

Statement 3 will be executed every time the loop has been executed.

For example

```
for (i = 0; i < 5; i++) {
    text += "The number is " + i + "<br>";
}
```

From this example, you can see that:

Statement 1 will set the variable before the loop begins (var i = 0).

Statement 2 will define the condition the loop needs to run (i should be lower than 5).

Statement 3 will increase a value (i++) whenever the code block that is in the loop is executed.

Statement 1

Typically, there will be a statement 1 that initializes the variable that is being used in the loop however, this may not always be the case. Statement 1 is not a requirement, it is optional. You can initiate several values, each separated by a comma in statement 1. For example:

```
for (i = 0, len = cars.length, text = ""; i < len; i++) {
    text += cars[i] + "<br>";
}
```

And, if you want, you can leave statement 1 out, especially if your values have been set before the loop begins:

```
var i = 4;
var len = cars.length;
var text = "";
for (; i < len; i++) {
    text += cars[i] + "<br>";
}
```

Statement 2

Statement 2 is used when you want to evaluate the condition of the first variable but this won't always be the case. Again, this is optional. If statement 2 evaluates true, the loop will begin again. If it evaluates false, the loop will stop.

If you leave statement 2 out, you need to put a break statement into the loop otherwise you will end up with an infinite loop, one that never ends and will crash

Statement 3

Usually, statement 3 is used to increment the value of the first variable but, again this may not always be the case and it is optional. Statement 3 is able to do pretty much anything – positive or negative increments, for example.

You can also leave statement 3 out, for example, if you were incrementing values in the loops:

```
var i = 0;
var len = cars.length;
for (; i < len; ) {
    text += cars[i] + "<br>";
    i++;
}
```

The For...In Loop

The for...in loop is used for looping through object properties:

For example:

```
var person = {fname:"Jane", lname:"Deer", age:26};
```

```
var text = "";
var x;
for (x in person) {
    text += person[x];
}
```

The While Loop

The while loop is used to loop through code blocks all the while a specific condition evaluates true. The syntax used is:

```
while (condition) {
    the code block that will be executed
}
```

For example:

In this example, the code that is in the loop is going to run repeatedly for as long as the variable called i is less than 8:

```
while (i < 8) {
    text += "The number is " + i;
    i++;
}
```

If you forget that the variable in the condition needs to be increased, the loop will never stop and your browser will crash

The Do...While Loop

The do...while loop is a variation of the while loop and will execute a block of code just once before it checks to see if the condition is evaluating true; at this point, the code will continue to loop until the condition evaluates false. The syntax used is:

```
do {
    that code that is going to be executed
}
while (condition);
```

For example:

The next example uses the do...while loop which will always execute once or more times regardless of whether the condition is true or false. This is because the condition is tested AFTER the block of code has been executed:

```
do {
    text += "The number is " + i;
    i++;
}
while (i < 8);
```

As before, don't forget that the variable in the condition needs to be increased or the loop will become infinite and will never end.

Comparing the For and While Loops

The while loop is pretty similar to the for loop with the exception that statements 1 and 3 are left out. This next example shows you a for loop in use to collect car names from the array called cars:

For example

```
var cars = ["Mercedes", "Ford", "Audi", "Opel"];
var i = 0;
var text = "";

for (;cars[i];) {
    text += cars[i] + "<br>";
    i++;
}
```

In this next example, the while loop is being used to collect the names of the cars from the array:

```
var cars = ["Mercedes", "Ford", "Audi", "Opel"];
var i = 0;
var text = "";
```

```
while (cars[i]) {
    text += cars[i] + "<br>";
    i++;
}
```

Exercises

Exercise 19

Change num1 to 2 and change num2 to 11 in the for loop and then run the code:

```
<!DOCTYPE html>

<html>

<body>


<p id="demo"></p>


<script>
var i;

for (i = num1; i < num2; i++) {

    document.getElementById("demo").innerHTML += i +
"<br>";

}

</script>

</body>
```

</html>

Exercise 20

Change the code so the loop begins counting at 4 and not 0:

```
<!DOCTYPE html>
<html>
<body>


<p id="demo"></p>


<script>
var i;
for (i = 0; i < 10; i++) {
    document.getElementById("demo").innerHTML += i + "<br>";
}
</script>


</body>
</html>
```

20 Questions to Test Your JavaScript Knowledge

1. Which of these is the right way to return the length of a string?
    - 'string',length
    - string,length
    - string.length
    - 'string'.length
2. Which of these is the right way to comment text?
    - // "the text" //
    - / "the text" /
    - */ "the text" /*
    - \\ "the text" \\
3. Which of these is the right way to log statements to the console?
    - consolelog("Hello world")
    - console.log("Hello world")
    - console.log{"Hello world"}
    - consolelog("Hello world")

4. Which of these is NOT a JavaScript comparator operator?

   - `<==`
   - `!==`
   - `===`
   - `>`

5. In an if statement, what comes after the expression?

   - curly braces
   - a colon
   - square brackets
   - brackets

6. Which of these statements will evaluate to false?

   - 'myName'.length > 2
   - 3 * 4 < 15
   - 4 / 2 == 2
   - 'inputControl'.length < 4

7. Which of these will return a value of 2?

   - 7 + 3 / 5
   - 'hi'.length - 1 * 2
   - (3 + 1) / 'hi'.length
   - 4 + (4 / 8)

8. What do we use the substring keyword for?

   - To create a string in a string
   - To return a partial part of a string
   - To re-order the characters within a string

- To substitute characters within a string

9. Which of these will return "he"?

   - 'hello world'.substring(1,2);
   - 'hello world'.(substring 1,2);
   - 'hello world'.substring(0,1);
   - 'hello world'.substring 0,1;

10. Which of these describes what functions are for?

    - To create a new variable
    - For math formulas
    - A reusable code that you can call on at any time in an application
    - To allow mathematical operators to be used

11. What is the input in a function known as?

    - function variable
    - parameter
    - return
    - global variable

12. Which of these is the right syntax for functions?

    - //1 var myFunction = function[] {};
    - //2 var myFunction = function() {};
    - //3 var myFunction = function{} ();
    - //4 var myFunction = function(); {};

13. Which of these is the right way to call the following function:

var multiplier = function(number) {

```
console.log(3 * number);

};
```

- multiplier 5 ;
- multiplier{5};
- multiplier(5);
- multiplier[5];

14. What does the return keyword do?

- It lets the output from one function be used somewhere else
- It lets a user go back to a previous code
- It logs output to the console
- It ends a statement in a function

15. Which of the following is the last condition for this for loop?

```
for (var condition = 0; condition < 5; condition ++) {

return condition;

};
```

- condition = 0
- condition ++
- return condition
- condition < 5

16. Which of these describes an array?

- A variable that is able to create functions

- A variable that is able to store lists of different data types separately
- A data type that is able to store data
- A data type that is able to create functions

17. Which of these is the right syntax for an array?
    - var array = [6; 7; "hello"];
    - var array = [6, 7, "hello"];
    - var array = { 6, 7 ,"hello"};
    - var array = { 6; 7; "hello"};

18. How do while loops differ from for loops?
    - The beginning of the while loop is not predefined
    - Comparison operators cannot be used by while loops
    - The end of the while loop is not predefined
    - The control of the loop in a for loop is not predefined

19. Which of these is not a JavaScript logical operator?
    - ||
    - &&
    - $$
    - !

20. Which of these is the correct symbol for the AND operator?
    - ||
    - &&

- $$

- !

Conclusion

Thank you again for purchasing this book!

I hope this book was able to help you understand JavaScript and what it is all about. Once you get into it, JavaScript is not a difficult language to learn; it just takes time, patience and concentration, not to mention perseverance.

The next step is to increase your learning. If you have understood everything in this book and scored high on the exercises and the quiz, you are ready to move on to more advanced programming concepts. If not, go back through the book and repeat it until you are certain you have got it.

Finally, if you enjoyed this book, then I'd like to ask you for a favor, would you be kind enough to leave a review for this book on Amazon? It'd be greatly appreciated!

Thank you and good luck!

Answers to Exercises

Exercise 1

```
<script>

var carName = "Ford";

document.getElementById("demo").innerHTML = carName;

</script>


</body>

</html>
```

Exercise 2

```
<script>

var number = 45;

document.getElementById("demo").innerHTML = number;

</script>


</body>

</html>
```

Exercise 3

```
<script>

var x = 15;

var y = 5;

document.getElementById("demo").innerHTML = x + y;

</script>



</body>

</html>
```

Exercise 4

```
<script>

var x = 10;

var y = 5;

document.getElementById("demo").innerHTML = x * y;

</script>



</body>

</html>
```

Exercise 5

```
<p id="demo"></p>



<script>

var x = 15;

x += 5;

document.getElementById("demo").innerHTML = x;

</script>



</body>

</html>
```

Exercise 6

```
<script>

var x = 15;

x -= 5;

document.getElementById("demo").innerHTML = x;

</script>
```

```
</body>
```

```
</html>
```

Exercise 7

```
<script>

document.getElementById("demo").innerHTML = 4 < 8;

</script>
```

```
</body>
```

```
</html>
```

Exercise 8

```
<script>

document.getElementById("demo").innerHTML = 12 != 6;

</script>
```

```
</body>
```

```
</html>
```

Exercise 9

```
<script>
```

```
if (4 > 3) {

    document.getElementById("demo").innerHTML = "Great
Job!";

}

</script>



</body>

</html>
```

Exercise 10

```
<script>

var firstName = "Jane";



if (firstName === "Deer") {

    document.getElementById("demo").innerHTML = "Hello
Jane!";

}

</script>
```

```
</body>

</html>
```

Exercise 11

```
</body>

</html>

<!DOCTYPE html>

<html>

<body>


<input id="myInput" type="text" value="Tutti Frutti">

<button onclick="checkFruit()">Check Fruit</button>

<p id="demo"></p>


<script>

function checkFruit() {

  var text;

  var fruits = document.getElementById("myInput").value;
```

```
switch(fruits) {

  case "Apple":

    text = "Apple's are good!";

    break;

  case "Banana":

    text = "I don't like Banana.";

    break;

  case "Satsuma":

    text = "Such a juicy Satsuma!";

    break;

  default:

    text = "That is a strange fruit!.";

}

document.getElementById("demo").innerHTML = text;

}

</script>


</body>
```

```
</html>
```

Exercise 12

```
<!DOCTYPE html>

<html>

<body>


<input id="myInput" type="text" value="Mercedes">

<button onclick="checkCar()">Check Car</button>

<p id="demo"></p>


<script>

function checkCar() {

  var text;

  var favCar = document.getElementById("myInput").value;


  switch(favCar) {

    case "Mercedes":

      text = "German car";
```

```
      break;
    case "Volvo":
      text = "Swedish car";

      break;
    case "Citroen":

      text = "French car";

      break;
    default:

      text = "Unknown car name";
  }

  document.getElementById("demo").innerHTML = text;
}

</script>


</body>

</html>
```

Exercise 13

```
<!DOCTYPE html>
```

```
<html>

<body>


<p id="demo"></p>


<script>

function myFunction() {

    document.getElementById("demo").innerHTML = "Hi
Guys!";

}

myFunction();

</script>


</body>

</html>
```

Exercise 14

```
<!DOCTYPE html>

<html>
```

```
<body>

<p id="demo"></p>

<script>

function myFunction() {

    return 10 * 10;

}

document.getElementById("demo").innerHTML =
myFunction();

</script>


</body>

</html>
```

Exercise 15

```
<!DOCTYPE html>

<html>

<body>
```

```
<p id="demo">The result is displayed here.</p>


<script>

var cars = ["Ford", "Mercedes", "Opel"];

document.getElementById("demo").innerHTML = cars;

</script>


</body>

</html>
```

Exercise 16

```
<!DOCTYPE html>

<html>

<body>


<p id="demo"></p>


<script>
```

```
var cars = ["Volvo", "Mercedes", "Opel"];

cars[o] = "Volvo";

document.getElementById("demo").innerHTML = cars;

</script>


</body>

</html>
```

Exercise 17:

```
<!DOCTYPE html>

<html>

<body>


<p id="demo"></p>


<script>

var fruits = ["Apple", "Banana", "Orange"];

fruits.pop();

document.getElementById("demo").innerHTML = fruits;
```

```
</script>
```

```
</body>
```

```
</html>
```

Exercise 18

```
<!DOCTYPE html>
```

```
<html>
```

```
<body>
```

```
<p id="demo"></p>
```

```
<script>
```

```
var fruits = ["Apple", "Banana", "Orange"];
```

```
fruits.push("Pineapple");
```

```
document.getElementById("demo").innerHTML = fruits;
```

```
</script>
```

```
</body>
```

</html>

Exercise 19

```html
<!DOCTYPE html>

<html>

<body>


<p id="demo"></p>


<script>

var i;

for (i = 2; i < 11; i++) {

    document.getElementById("demo").innerHTML += i +
"<br>";

}

</script>


</body>

</html>
```

Exercise 20

```
<!DOCTYPE html>

<html>

<body>


<p id="demo"></p>


<script>

var i;

for (i = 4; i < 10; i++) {

    document.getElementById("demo").innerHTML += i +
"<br>";

}

</script>


</body>

</html>
```

Answers to JavaScript Quiz

1. 'string'.length
2. // "the text" //
3. console.log("Hello world")
4. <==
5. curly braces
6. 'inputControl'.length < 4
7. (3 + 1) / 'hi'.length
8. To return a partial part of a string
9. 'hello world'.substring(0,1);
10. A reusable code that you can call on at any time in an application
11. Parameter
12. //2 var myFunction = function() {};
13. multiplier(5);
14. It lets the output from one function be used somewhere else
15. condition < 5
16. A variable that is able to store lists of different data types separately
17. var array = [5, 6, "hello"];
18. The end of the while loop is not predefined
19. $$
20. &&

Made in the USA
Middletown, DE
15 November 2017